THE MISEDUCATION OF **EMOTION**

Book of poems

R. L. WRIGHT JR.

THE
MISEDUCATION OF
EMOTION
R. L. Wright Jr.
© 2023 Xalt Publishing/ R. L. Wright Jr.

Published by:
Xalt Publishing
Cover Design:
Xalt Studios

ISBN 979-8-35091-616-4

Dedicated to

The beautiful Asia-Bryanne
The beautiful Zora Leona
My loving parents Elaina & Robert Sr.
The dopest Marlaina & Delaun
My supporting family members
&
My Real Friends

Contents

INTRO

In the following narrative, we meet a wise individual who made a significant discovery about the importance of understanding emotions in maintaining good mental health. Understanding the importance of identifying and processing one's emotions, this individual recognized the key to leading a happy and fulfilling life. With the belief that anyone can learn to manage their emotions and live a more peaceful and contented life through self-reflection and understanding, they shared their thoughts. I'm the person being referred to.

By creatively writing words on a page, I have the ability to convey my thoughts to another person who may read my work at a different time and place. This allows them to gain insight into my state of mind at the moment I wrote each poem. Although I'm not physically present, you will be able to perceive my emotions. In this collection, you will find a blend of my older poetry and some that I have written as recently as a week before its release. It is a combination of emotions that I have experienced or witnessed delivered through poetic storytelling.

As I worked on collecting my poetry, I realized that it could be something more than I had ever dreamed of publishing. I initially struggled with figuring out what I was doing. By taking a step back, I was able to write more. In the final stages of my project, I came to the realization that my poetry was all over the place yet still displayed a strong sense of passion. I decided to develop something that would capture the essence of emotion. We all share the same emotions, despite our differences. This common thread binds us together as human beings.

Having said that, I would now like to introduce you to

"The Miseducation of Emotion."

[I may not be a master of poetry,
but my heart spills forth in poetic expression.]

Following Shadows

Flower Girl

My dear queen,
We gave birth to a little you!
My dear Princess,
I cherish how much you've grown.
I will be your wings every single time that you fall.
Your rock!
Your pillar!
That foundation that keeps you so strong.

I will always be your number one fan.
Your most passionate supporter.
No one could ever replace you.
And no other individual has the right to mine.
I'm your father
and I'm grateful for the adventure.

Theta Psi

We may seem small.
Thoroughly trained for it all.
Our bonds are strong.
Our soil is rich.
History runs so deep.
Peep the hall of science.
The war recapitulates
the bloodline of royalty.
Mighty purple and gold
Students of her language
We pledge to her
A marriage, oh so strong
She protects us from far away,
Her knowledge gives us shelter.
But cook owts are a wreck.
Friends are made.
We teach our young-ins.
To groom the young ins
Be a beacon of hope.
Trust the process.
Complete the process.
Theta Psi to the bone
Only a century
Man, the machine!
Omega, roll-on

One Night Stand

So many words
So many thoughts
I pressure myself.
As I choke on what to say
nothing average
Nothing plain
But special
from deep within
Willing to go the extra mile
To surmount the words
That simply harasses
the courage of my feelings.
Which is not sprung
But a skyrocket of like
A pocketful of smiles
rosy cheeks of lust
A journey within my inner empathy
To surface enchanting thoughts
Provocative words fill my mind.
But this isn't about sex.
This is different mi amor.
This is the derivation of...
Love

WRITTEN 2012

Hot Take

They treat me like an exfoliation.
Because my brain travels with disassociation,
to the real world.
Self-confidence is a real pearl.
Buried in the outer walls of a depression swirl

Double standards are the motivation.
Now let's spin the curl.

They judge you like the police.
That fills the station.
To fund a vacation
Robbing the nation
Supported by the foundation
of Christian correlation.

Bashing the cops is not my angle.
at this moment
It's the hypocrites.
The ones that tell you to be holly
but don't give a shit!
Until it affects their pockets,
Their image,
Their way of living
Right?

You are the one who's depressed.
And it's sometimes cloaked.
Now that you've invoked
The clip that smoked.
The last one that joked
on me that I left soaked!

Now keep those words that you stroked.
And choked to get yoked
by your pastor,
to yourself.

UNWRITTEN APPROVAL

Mask are worn in many different situations,
For pursuance,
of who we want to be.
When it's hard to see,
Creatively,
that you want to breathe!

But

Mask are worn in many situations,
For pursuance,
Of security.
If I speak,
you speak! So, I write this poetry
because it doesn't fuss back.
Words that don't define comprehension.
Words that only draw blood.
You must defend your peace.
At the cost of my piece of mine.
Frustrations of a verbal chest match
That all stems from opinion.

But

Mask are worn in different situations,
For progression.
When I open my eyes,
After dreams of misery,
Perfection is shown.
With no sign of gloom,
But with the price to pay
of becoming an artist.
My words are used to manipulate.
The colors of life
To maintain iconic.
When my actions are quite moronic.

But

Mask are worn in different situations,
For depression.

A Smile

Happy or not!
When you see me what do you think?
Do you think I'm happy because of my smile?
Happy because of the goofiness?
The laughter I bring to the plate?
If you pitched a curve ball
Id surly strike out
My smile is nothing but a front.
A put on.
A showboat
I smile out of the pain of life.
I feel life jump and gain.
Each smile is pain that stains
the fresh white carpet of my heart
Part of the young man you see goofing.
Goofing with a smile
Which is no pure style
I am nothing I am trash.
I was born alone, and I will die alone
I'm bitter.
Heartless and could give a damn what anyone thinks.
I'm cold.
So cold that it hurts.
Smiling is nothing.
Without meaning from the heart
My smile is irregular.
Jejune to happiness
Truculent to life so I die at a young age.
I'm dead and there's no coming back.

WRITTEN 2003

"sigh"

Crazy crave for more than physical attraction.
A desire for beautiful words
coupled with actions
Sometimes the heart beats
for genuine affection
All that is wanted is a complete connection
Lost in the deepest depths of conversation
Because I don't want this moment to end

LESS OXYGEN

Just a sliver of insecurity
More than enough to ignite a wave of panic....
Pulsing with the intensity of a runaway train
Bringing someone to a complete and utter halt
Till such time as one's dreams
Got trapped someplace deep!
Deep beneath the aftermath of the event
And thus, their uncertainty
becomes the inheritance of anxiety.

Bang Bang

My spirit is hungry.
Secluded. I emerged from battle.
Wounds on both sides. I never use the term "hate."
However, it is too late.

For you!

Only one memory springs to mind.
As I analyze your features...

You're an embarrassment,
creating a repulsive
bitterness in my mouth...

My passion is fueled by my suffering...

Icy walls surrounded my soul.
In my core,
my deepest aspirations,
from top to bottom.
I "AM" an eye for an eye.

You provoked hostilities.
With a strategy for a speedy retreat,
not in this scenario.
I will crush you.

You see closer to your dreams,
I see closer to you'll never wake up.
It's business as usual.
Nothing personal, chump.

Rather, you should take caution with those words.
Your words!
Because I'm coming!

Can we talk?

Shorty, I believe in you!
You're so beautiful!
But let me actually get at you.
I know you've been through a lot.
And I can see the world of hurt he left you in.

The real beauty is seeing every fucked-up
crack and bruise on your heart.
See this heart of mine comes from darker times.
I fought like hell to win me back.
But this is where connections are made.

Those cracks never fully heal.
They tell your stories.
Within those stories
is someone thirsting to love again.
wanting the pain to become numb
And all the broken pieces to become invisible.
To the next

As I open her door

The power of mind control
Thoughts with happy sights
Zombified thinking of all peace
Has taken over
Lust with magnitudes
that transition brain waves
This is no witchery
It is simply falling for a woman

Creed

She said you're a temptation.
Caused by a sensation
But you just want to stick your location.
In my destination
Which leads to an increased population
of the next generation!
So, no need for explanation
Or a demonstration

Me: "Cute"

I love how you love yourself.
Don't let lust woo you.
Chambering strength
To embrace the light
of the candle lit deep within.

My taste in words
awakens her every thought
She said, "you spitting."
moments later She dropped her addy.

All my ex's live in Texas

You said you love me
But we were young
So young that we thought our love was right
Wrong we were,
in countless ways.
Nightly climbing through your window
So, you could become my first.
In the car, my brother naps,
So young, yet mission accomplished,
perhaps.
Scaling the window,
Of the daughter who's voice I heard,
In church on Sunday.

Ain't that something

I grew
and so did my morals
But youth is ignorance.
She was Dawn.
When she caught my attention
All she wanted was love
That wasn't me
All she wanted was to go to prom
That wasn't her to be;
Who I chose to hold my palm
She cried
But I was still her lip balm
Until I found another
Another so damaging

Damn.

Lauren was karma.
Early 20's was meant to be a party
When we tried to play house
We wasn't ready for that shit
Instead broke each other down.

She was a firecracker
And sometimes we had fiery conversations
My character was young
I was clingy doing the most
To be her hero.
We are in love
but too young to grow together

The small chunk removed from my heart
Next to the memory of our relationship
Is what grew me up
I watched you walk away from me
The greatest pain I've ever known

LA FAMILIA

My family looks at me like I'm a leader.
I'm just trying to give them
a close face to believe in
They taught me to play the game.
To change the game
They don't even ask for sh*t!

They just want me to be great.
excel with my dreams
All my life, they helped fund it.
They believe in me.
Now I made it
We made it!
No matter who turns their back on us,
I'll never turn my back on us!

As a young boy, I grew a high-top fade.
I'm a 90s baby.
My cousin told me I would grow to be great.

Los, look at me now!
Spiritually connected
He's still taking bullets for me.
Making sure I can get by
like the old days 100 degrees in the wintertime.
Texaco runs
Arizona teas with a mango vibe.

My family deserves this
I have another cousin.
born the same day as me
age the same as me.
Our journeys are different
but our hearts are aligned.
This is for those members with no voice.
And can't find a spark in the dark
All I needed was time.
Now sip your wine.

SADE

Sashaying Sade
She's sophisticatedly
Silly, Sexy,
Sometimes selfish
Shooting shots
Slowly smoking
Shotgun spitting
soldiers saving
Sniper survivors
Sean's skull split
Seven stitches
Securing secrets
Sitting seaside
Shaking sickly
Slightly strange
Stealthy swans

STORY TIME

It became a joke in our friendship, surrounded by a million other stupid inside jokes that made us both crack up laughing like the kids we almost were. "Hey, marry me, Nora!" I would call out, and she'd punch me in the arm, and we'd flirt like we had when we were sixteen-year-old neighbors who didn't know any better. Instead, we were graduating from college.

If I brought her food from her favorite place to eat and delivered it to her when she'd had one too many drinks the night before, she'd mumble, "Marry me, dude," against the pillow, her eyes still half shut.

As she gracefully moves her legs off the couch, making space for him to sit, she leans into him with such tenderness that it warms his heart. With a sweet smile, she whispers my name: "Oh, James." Marry me."

When I said it in front of my family, I caught a weird look flitting across my mother's face, disappearing in an instant. "Stop playing with me," she said, giving me a playful punch on the arm. I blew her a kiss, and we were reprimanded for acting inappropriately at the table, our cheeks flushed with lust.

Our friends had a similar reaction. They only laughed when Nora and I started laughing about it; before then, it was just James saying, "Marry me, Nora!" into a room full of considerate silence. It felt like everybody was waiting for something, but I didn't know what. I told a joke instead.

We were sitting in my car, about to drive home, when she said something about it. "I'm going to make it weird. I'll stop asking soon, I promise." My voice was uncharacteristically soft.

Even though I didn't say it, she knew what I meant. I was talking about the looks on our friends' faces when I jokingly asked her to marry me—that smug expression like they knew more than we did. The weird way the silence had hung in the room.

I looked at her, with her almond-brown eyes and the glow across her face. I looked at her beautiful curly hair, her long eyelashes, and the way his front tooth was just a little bit crooked because she refused to wear his retainer even after suffering through braces for two years.

"James," she whispered, her voice trying to hide in her throat. "Don't stop asking."

It took me a moment to react. I couldn't help but smile when I saw her looking at me with a glimmer in her eyes. "Yeah?"

"Yeah," she answered, and then turned the radio up so that the Beyonce song that's on repeat blasted through the car. I grabbed her hand and laughed, throwing my head back. We drove, just like we always had, singing, and talking about nothing at all.

She wanted me to keep asking, even though it didn't feel like a joke anymore. She kept responding with laughter, a change of subject, or an invitation to nap together for now. One day, though, I thought her answer would be different. What I thought in the car was:

"I'll keep asking because I believe that one day she'll say yes, and I can't wait for that moment."

Love is a drug.

The last embrace we shared,
Did you feel the vibrations bared?
Pounding my chest with such force,
a feeling that I cannot divorce.

A love so deep,
It longed to be expressed,
But fear and doubt kept it repressed.

Locked away,
hidden from view,
longing to be shared with you.

My heart,
It tends to obsess,
So, I must keep things in check,
no less.

I had to keep it that way,
To ensure my emotions
Stay calm and don't stray!

Wrong Turn

My ex drove me to depression,
It was a long walk back.
To a pack of wolves in the tree
I gave up a limb.
It was either that or it was me.
I had no more heart to give!
I belonged to many others.

Wolf after wolf,
They became tattoos on my soul.
As I walked down this path
The new ink became old.

I met another passenger.
She gave me flutters.
I had to lace up.

We both had drawn scars.
But hers came with a light.
Every word she spoke
It was like the sun overpowering the clouds.
I'm not going to lie,
She would be better off with another traveler with less bags,
But we are beautiful!

Happily, ever after...ish

You tried to change them, huh?
Held your tongue more?
Attempted to be Friendlier,
more attractive,
less impulsive?

Well, I'm sorry to tell you
But humans are not homes.
The fairy tales were wrong.

Some prince charming was only charm
And some princess wanted to be saved from
behind an unlocked door.

I wish they told us that
Instead, they spill stories of perfect love.
No one leaves without being chased
Toxic love!

If they want to leave
Let em leave.
Take time to get stronger.
It won't be easy.
But we are beautiful.
And that's something
Not every soul knows how to love.

Upgrade

Within the mirror of one's purity,
I recognize my missteps reflected.
Self-inflicted lessons
That is the true cruelty within me.
However,
Once more, I will ascend.
From debris to blaze
Jolted into an eternal state of motivation.
From a name with no significance
over towards the pinnacle of a prefix.

Life's balance

Let me tell you something baby.
I OOZEE space charisma!
From within me flows
a certain charm and grace
Radiating outwards.

Long walks on the beach,
might not be my thing.
I'm a southern boy!

I want to grasp your hand,
To feel its warmth and understand,
The comfort that it brings to you,
A simple touch,
so sweet and free.
then lift it up with grace.

In the glow of the night,
I spin you around,
Lost in the moment,
Our feet levitate the ground.

Gazing deep into your being,
A journey through your essence.
Exploring the depths of your whole,
Discovering the secrets of your soul.

All this just to express the beauty that you possess.
Words cannot do justice,
Your glow is like the sun shining brightly,
second to none.

Your eyes sparkle like the stars
Guiding me through life's memoirs
Your smile is like a ray of light Bringing joy.
You are beautiful; that much is true.
and I am grateful to know you.

South side the realist

Greatly awaken,
coming out of Dallas.
I read "To live life is to wake up to a beautiful host."
Hmm, not this world!
In this world
Everything is about hitting a lic with a gloc
or being famous on the app isn't worth a tic on the toc!

Our generation wakes up to plan a post.
Social media is compared to crack cocaine.
Who are we to be ashamed...
of the 80s

The digital mindfuck of cellular devices
Allows infectious information
to spread like rabies

Now adult babies
with rabies
grow up taking for granted
the mechanics of how to cursively write,

I bet they can tell you what rappers are OWNED
by Sprite.
Despite my negativity,
some grow up right...

SILK

Repeatedly,
I fall in love
with the conception of romantic love.
Emotional nineties RnB
while sitting in the shower.
Imagining holding one another in the rain.
You know,
OG love shit.

The Perfect Stranger

Insane conversations
across the bar seem so prefab
Looming a morning rehab
from an accelerator
originally in the moment
we celebrate with confetti.
Verbally, sexually petty
because of the glow of your charisma
echoing, which is an enigma
that cannot be pardon
Youthful Lust when our souls entangle in arson
umbering aroma
as our lips touch for a magical persona.

—Love,
Tequila

Pat-Ron

Throughout the earlier parts of the morning,
When I opened my eyes to see you there.
As I sober up
I thought to myself,
Who tf are you?

Lucky

To be lucky is to discover
A hopeless romantic with a dirty mind
Much kinkier than picking a four-leaf clover
This is a gem you cherish.
A treasure that will cater to your needs,
kiss you where it hurts,
and until it hurts.

Your sexual checkmate
that not only turns you on,
But takes a trip through a toy chest.
That will have you dreaming
about your organism.

COUGAR

I used to think
to court an older woman
was to be loved by an experienced woman
to be understood
To be a sex puppet

But I now see
Courting an older woman
Wouldn't Help
Groom me
I used to willingly
Throw myself in the line of fire.
because I know
What it's like to burn someone
Younger

My words were weapons.
Like a lethal injection
Injecting her soul with my toxic ways.
Having you lovesick for days
When all you wanted was change.

WRITTEN 2013

Murder for a jar of red ruM

We treated him like family.
But he was never biological.
I wanted to get the job done.
But that's neurological.
I woke up from a dream.

and tried to go back and finish it.
Only rules apply.
Never depend on a codependent.

When he got out of jail,
the first person he seen
Was the last person he seen
My mama always said I had a choice.
Which is as humble as it come.

I dream angry
So, I crashed his funeral.
His family was grieving.
but I'm here for a plate.
They know I did it!
Rowdy and want me to leave.

I spit in his casket.
I lifted my bottle and gave a toast.
"An eye for an eye!"
"This body was for Los."
Before I can finish,
I'm facing multiple straps.

I thought
"fcuk it!"
"We can get to shooting like we hooping."

Like a running back
I tote that thing.
Colliding with linebackers
Death-defying moment

KISS

My breath is short.
Chest full of pain.
Some sort of pressure
My heart speaks a different language.
Rampage raging
regardless rules
Vision of grateful blur
As I laugh now and cry later.
Arm pins
Leg needles
Life isn't over.
This isn't the last breath.

WRITTEN 2012; REVISED 2020

Death

Such a peculiar five letter word
Expresses the heavy weight of peace
A drug so severe
That all pain is relieved
Life is left behind
All joy is sorrow
Next, it's court
They promise no tomorrow
Last, it's the judge
Either horn or halo
as my head weakens
Lowered down
I've suffered enough, my lord
Take me now

WRITTEN 2012

To the lovely couple

Good evening, ladies, and Gentlemen,

I want to start with a big thank you to our friends and family for being here with us on the special day of my sister's wedding. I am Brandon, and I am Nora's brother. I am honored to speak some lines on this amazing day of our life. I would like to welcome you all and thank you for celebrating her special day with us.

It is too hard for me to find the right words for expressing my feelings. I'm honored to take care of my lovely sister and support her at her wedding. I am so blessed to be standing here today in front of all our friends and family, celebrating our happiness together.

My love for my sister is very precious, and I am a lucky brother for taking care of my twin sister. Since my childhood, I have had memorable fun moments with my sister. It's a bond of love behind our fights and laughter. My sister Nora is my best friend. We had lots of fights, and I will miss everything about her. Hearing about your wedding, I felt sad about leaving your home. I can't express how much it means to have a sister like you. I am your support by standing at your side. You are always my strength in tough times.

If getting married had not been important, I would never have let my sweet sister leave this home. From the first time I met James I believed, you both are made for each other, and your kind nature realized me that you would be a special person in Nora's life after Me. We would like to welcome you into our family. You have a kind nature, and you are the best for my sister in all aspects. I am very happy for my lovely sister. As a brother, I request James to take care of my sister. Wishing the very best life to the bride and groom for a lifetime of forever blooming love.

Lots of best wishes for starting your new life together. May this be the start of your happiness. You are always perfect as a twin and now you are an amazing wife too. You always deserve the best in your life. Many best wishes to both of you for starting a new, long, and happy future together.

I Love you Nora and James. Thank you for being together.

Cycle

When a man tells you he loves you,
Being here wasn't in his plans.
It takes time for that love to grow.
Sometimes a feeling that is pure,
a feeling that is genuine.
Sometimes actions that contradict,
actions that are lustful.

He wants you to believe in him.
Trust is a dice roll.
What a man lacks in the early stages.
Is a flick of flaw.
A man can be kind.
A man can listen
A man can be romantic.
But
A man can't sometimes express himself,
in the brightest of lights.
When it's his stage
Behind the scenes, never seem so perfect.

When a man says, "I love you,"
He's really saying, be patient.
Triumph, his triumph
Even Superman turns into Clark Kent.
His imperfections will soon come to light.
Arguments will be tough.
Without them, there is no adversity.
With them, you know who you're dealing with.

Glow

Fueling every confident man is a woman.
Or better,
fueling every Confident man ought to be you!
and yet every man must accept.
Not in my life, another.
I mean another life.
Perhaps don't even worry about it.
I'm privileged,
I'm the guy!

Experiencing you in my life
has become one of my crowning achievements.
Recognizing I have degrees
but Damn!
Debate you?
To fancy paper?
Paper, I paid for?

Well yeah, I worked hard for this paper.
But such paper doesn't bring me joy
when I'm sad
when I'm down.
Simply having you around
when circumstances are... hard.
That paper offers me prestige
but you offer permanence!

You are my obsession.
My pillow and linens
Every embrace I appreciate your grip so tightly.
You are my solar energy
keeping my night sky glowing
inspiring me to never let my ego take control.

You are my closest companion.
My person,
my best friend!
I've honestly believed the expression,
"Best friend"
for you, Was injustice
So, I wifed you!

Zeus

Born for power
trained for greatness
Arrogance spreads throughout my heart.
With a gift from the gods
Magnetically connecting
sparks to my brain
with a rush never felt before

Mortals would be diseased.
A Demi, severely injured
This is no amateur power.
I've grown to fill my straps well.
Looking down upon life
They speak of me in fear.
Sending up prayers
But I laugh thunder
And wink darts of lightning
In response

My first line of defense is Ares.
Though no one bothers
I sit on Mount Olympus.
Eventually, taking sore
to populate

Alignment

Exceeded my expectations a while ago.
Didn't know what I was writing for.
With my voice
Let me live without any breaths.
Remember my teachings.
Money don't change people.
It brings out who they really are.
Train your mind
to help shape the new generation.
I see you with my third eye.
You imposter's.

Double Edge

They tell you to be strong.
Be the man of the house.
Don't forget to play sports.
That's the only way out.
We sleep seven to a crib.
With no college degrees.
They preach education.
Rack up a bill for the C's.

THE GAME

School is cool!
School is what you make it!
Semesters build!
All you need is a seed.
In the soil!
So that you can learn how to eat,
Now enjoy the show!

Boy Scouts

Good ole-boys,
The states d-line.
You thugs!
An organized gang
That gets the support.
Camouflaged
All lives matter, huh?
Hiding in plain sight
while protesters scream
You piece of shit,
Stop killing our people!
But back to the subject of matter.
Murders!

Not all icons should be judged by their looks.
But the murders in blue
need to be in the blues
Without the chest-wide S.

And they say, "protect."
Your people
Instead, you neglect
Your people
Because we rep a different set.

Your actions ally with the oppressor.
Like we are the cattle
and you are the flesher.
If trees could talk, they'd talk for days.
Not breaking under tremendous pressure.

Creating the pencil that I put to this book
To educate you on the memories of our thresher
ancestors.

Bullying

Brandon walks home crying.
Unpleasant thoughts defying sanity
thinking of the names equivalent to "ugly" and "fat"
flooding his lug and adding names to meet his bat.

Bad vibrations
He thought no one would care to listen.
His father was tough.
Didn't notice a glistening
His mother was rough.
But sat down to harp
he he-he's, ha-ha's, and ja-ja's
  "Mama, the pressure is too much."
  "Son, you're a child. What could you possibly find hard to
  stomach?"
  "Life, mama, we are different. I PRAY WE don't PLUMMET."
He slams the door.
Covered in fear
of his freedom
His bat wasn't enough.
Ash covered his cheek from his last tear.

Deposit

You give me pain.
I turn it into strength.
They doubt me, and I show them who I am.
Throw insults at me,
although you're not what you pretend to be.

You waste your energy.
I can't be beaten.
Not because I am untouchable,
But because I don't combat with fools.
I'll dance with my nemesis,
then drown him in his own wickedness.

Never will I take the bait.
My reflection is far worse.
Blaze in your own flames,
for you are your own tragedy.

SADE (PART I)

That's when it occurred.
She was detained.
Her ankles were bound

A dreadful crime,
So cruel and vile.
no escaping,
Pleading, begging for pardon
Just a stillness,
A quiet acceptance.

24 hours earlier,
Towards the end of business,
She met her spouse,
Whose clock-watching won.
She came near,
without his knowing why

Her lips met his in a fiery kiss,
Straddling his lap with a daring bliss.
Adorned in just a trench coat,

Softly spoken,
        "Be home by ten."
Flushed cheeks
as he waved goodbye.

He'd say he's working late,
A phrase oft repeated without debate.
He roamed far and wide,
Never staying in one place.
His home was the open road,
never came home to an endless space.

A child they mourn,
Whose life was brief,
Whose absence now,
Brings endless grief.
his name was Brandon.

Alone Nora stood,
with none to lean upon.
Silent and still she sat,
A weight upon her heart,
Sorrow etched upon her face,
Tears threatening to start.
Nightly she waits,
Till her breaking point she hits.

Late he was,
And home he came,
Not until the early morning.

Branches Fall

I received a gift from her cousin,
a cousin I didn't really know.
I heard she was trash and was fast.
I heard it from a friend in passing,
so, I let it go.

It turned out not to be a gift.
But a rather unfortunate message
They said she wanted nothing to do with me.
Out of confusion, I grew livid.

I argued back and forth.
Trying to plead my case.
A case that wasn't meant for me to understand.

My goodness gracious!
This is the day I found out about you.
No one mentioned the news was precious.
She said:
    "There was a baby."
Me:
    "WAS a baby?"
Her:
    "Yes! "Man WTF!""Is it mine?"
Her:
    "It WAS yours!"

Damn, this was tough!

My heart was broken, raging, livid.
I couldn't have you.
I couldn't hold you,
I could only reminisce.

We were young.
Relationship dumb!
She didn't know what to do.
I got advice from a bum!
The exit price was you.

She never had the heart to tell me,
so, the message was relayed.
I couldn't sleep.
I broke down on my knees.
All I could do was weep.

To my daughter, my son,
my unborn love.
You never had a chance
to become what you would.
Forgive your father.
I hate your mother!
I had no say
and we broke up for good.

You were a gift sent to me.
But I never got to meet you.
I was robed!
A branch fell from my tree.

WRITTEN 2013

Deception

Lies!
More than twice
Now a breath of life
No regular life,
but your life
If confirmed
then bleeds the heart.

My love demands
point approval.
Tension surmounts
the room
with sorrowful pauses
remaining answers of bullshit

Black Fragments

The lies don't offend me,
But I must admit, I defend me.
Either you ridding shotty,
Or are you racing against me?
Sitting in the back creates hidden envy.
Excuse me for being paranoid.
That's just the blackness in me.

My cousin was shot in the back.
By his best friend now serving life,
God saved him.
Those were the best odds on his dice.

Back in the day,
they had real friendships.
Now clout infects the character;
of the narrator.

They wasn't there for the pain.
But benefit from the expenses,
defenseless against the impulsive,
relentless,
Pretentious,
friendless back seat covers.

Deep in my soul,
I thought we were brethren for life.
But yall boys not loyal and trail with a knife.
Fake friends never play fair.
We grew up on broken fragments.
Fake friends never care,
But try to remain stagnant.

SADE (PART II)

Little did he know,
What fate had in store,
A path unknown,
Lay ahead to explore.

His world, once steady and secure,
Now teeters on the brink,
A universe about to flip,
And leave him on the without

His cherish, so dear and true,
He cannot keep.

Preservation is his only choice,
To honor and value with a voice.

Up to date
Sade, the new assistant,
wrapping up her tasks for the day.
Nora, his wife,
Requested him to have her escorted away.

No issue at all,
That's what they said,
No trouble to recall,
No need to dread.

A usual occurrence,
Nothing out of the ordinary.
They walked away,
Both of them,
Silent and solemn.

Sade's gaze fixed upon Nora,
A curious interest in her eyes.
She asked if the weapon was acquired,

And with a nod,
it was in possession.

As Nora slid on her sunglasses,
She retreated further into the privacy of her hood.
With a firm hold on her purse.

Ahead of each vehicle they went,
Moving forward with intent.
Both individuals,
looking for rooms to explore next door.

Sade ascends with grace,
Nora lags, a slower pace.
Anxious yet assured,
Her goal is clear and pure.
To get the job done,
Her determination won't be outdone.

Upon entering the room
the air was thick with soft scent
And shadows danced in discontent.
she wondered what lay hidden there
And felt a shiver in the air
But still I pressed on through the dark

A fume lit up,
A flame danced in the air.
A moment of warmth, A flicker of flare.

Nora waited, Awaiting direction,
Further steps to take, In patient reflection.

In moments fleeting,
Sade did change,
Her outfit swapped,
a sight so strange
In Nora's belly,
a flutter grew,
A feeling that was strange and new.
Self-assurance dwindled,
Her confidence, unkindled.

Fixated on the tool,
Her gaze unwavering,
Lost in its power, Her mind unrelenting.
She stood there, pondering,
Could she handle it, she wondered.

Sade spoke with authority,
Her words demanded attention,
        "Listen to me!"
        "Go and stand, over there"
        "Shed your coat, let it fall to the floor."
        "You're under arrest!"
Nora asked,
        "For what purpose?"
Sade:
        "For attempted murder"
        "Give me the bag now;"
        "Where is the weapon?"
Sade, dressed in blue,
A cop's uniform, brand new.
Nora was shook
She's caught on the line,
A fish on the hook,
Trapped in a moment,
Unable to look.

Her wrist,
lifted high,
A graceful motion in the sky.

Sade handcuffed her,
And uttered these words with care,
      "Wait right there," she said with flair.

That's when it occurred.
She was detained.
Her ankles were bound

A dreadful crime,
So cruel and vile.
no escaping,
Pleading, begging for pardon
Just a stillness,
A quiet acceptance.

Nora spoke,
      "You don't need these."
      "Make love to me,
      Let our bodies entwine,
      In passionate ecstasy."
      "Kiss me while you fuck me!"
Sade responded,
      "You're here for my pleasure."
      "Not for yours."
      "That's different," said Nora,

Her words were brief and clear,
A simple observation,
But one that we all could hear.

Sade's hand stretched out,
Towards Nora's bag,
A moment of hesitation,
Before she could grab.

Here's Your Cake

Your selfish!
To let me live a life of sacrifice.
While he benefits
The truth doesn't live within you.

25 years of marriage
To ruin what I thought
was loves perfect kiss.
To give him hope
While I give you freedom
Is it selfish of me?
To want a kingdom

To disregard my feelings
Night after night
I crave you.
Fight after fight
But you crave him.
Despite
Turning me down with all of your might.

I want you to love me
But your focus on self
I satisfy you.
But you play Santa's elf.
We are both selfish.
But it's now time for you to leave.
You know
I can see so clearly.
Goodwill has your bags.

sincerely,

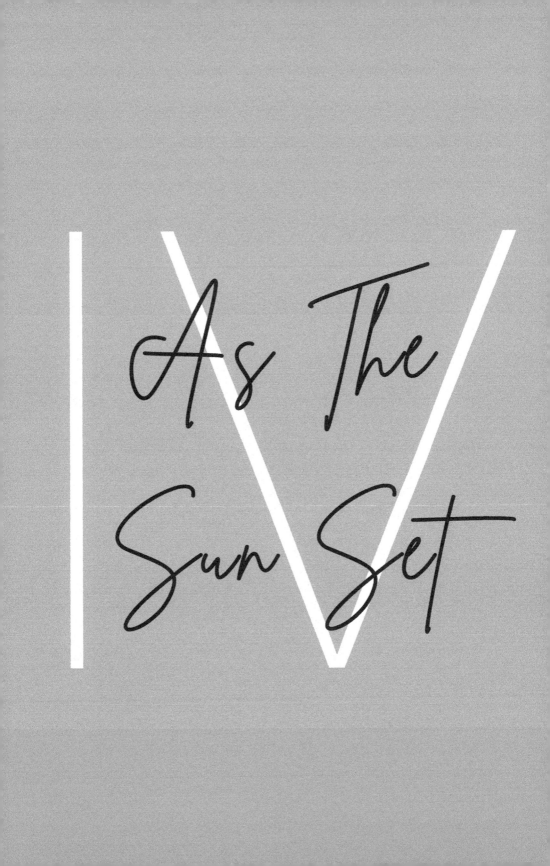

IV

As The

Sun Set

STORY TIME

Sade had never liked my husband. "He doesn't appreciate you," she mumbled one day through a mouthful of sushi. "He takes you for granted, Nora."

At the time, I insisted that she was wrong. My husband, James, was a wonderful man, and I felt like I'd notice if he didn't appreciate me—wouldn't I? Still, that conversation planted a seed in my brain, which quietly grew and began to smother my relationship.

I started to overthink. Was he taking me for granted? When I brought it up to Sade, she reached out a hand and gently squeezed my arm. "I didn't want to say anything earlier, but I think maybe he's seeing someone else."

The words sank into my stomach like a stone in a cold lake. Sade had to be wrong; my husband had always been faithful. After that conversation, I started to examine every interaction I had with my husband. When he leaned away from a kiss and pressed his lips to my cheek instead; when he told me he was too tired at night and rolled over to sleep.

The idea made me feel sick. Our wedding day had been the best day of my life, full of light and hope for the future. James was my soulmate, my everything. Just the fact that he existed has always given me hope for the future. Sometimes, I caught him looking at me like I was a stranger. There was no fondness left in his eyes.

I spent more time with Sade, who was eager to comfort me. She took me out for drinks, set up The Best Man Holiday on her TV, and made popcorn. Sade was willing to call me at any hour of the night. She was my rock as my heart began to freeze over. I felt myself slowly fall out of love with the person who I was sure had betrayed me.

I got the divorce papers ready because Sade thought it would be best to shock James with them, hopefully pushing him to admit that he had been unfaithful. Sade helped me every step of the way, and I felt a sense of relief at being able to finally leave the purgatory I had been living in. My husband insisted there was nothing wrong, but I knew otherwise. That's why I broke every rule in the relationship handbook and went through his phone while he was sleeping.

No matter how hard I searched, there were no emails from dating sites or texts from affair partners. If he was cheating on me, he would have scrubbed every piece of evidence from his phone. I almost put the phone down, but then I saw a message preview from several months ago that made my heart stumble in my chest. Thinking I must be mistaken, I clicked on the conversation.

SADE: I think that Nora might be having an affair. She takes you for granted, James. She doesn't appreciate you.

SADE: But I do.

Protect Love

Once I've entrusted my heart,
commit to understanding it.
develop it.
listen to its experiences.
Feel how cold it is.
The grief.
Desire.
The affection and empathy that formed it.
But please avoid damaging it.

A Glimpse of Depression

The few days you get
to see the ones you love,
If that feeling is mutual,
let them know.
If you aren't feeling the same way,
Let them go.

Before they let themselves go.
Lies have only left endless trails of voices.
Voices of self-sabotage,
promising me another life,
Depending on how quick I end this one.

This life is a mirage.
I've had to cleave to my mind to make choices.
I have had to learn not to trust my mind.

Mind or instinct?
I can't tell them apart.
I know for sure these voices make a promise,
And what difference would it make
if they also broke this one.

Only more reason I need to restart.
Let's look at the recap.
Why am I standing at the edge of this cliff?
This head talks.

It keeps repeating all those negative thoughts.
My best try is a what if?
What if I jumped and hugged these rocks?
Well, I bet that'd be the only felt affection.
The only affection I've felt since I was nineteen.

When my aunt died
my feelings died with her.
When my cousin left
there were no feelings
left for me to chase him with.

I asked God why we all couldn't
just stay alive forever.
The voices said nothing.

It had gotten harder to bear with
And even relationships couldn't be intoxicant,
How would their words didn't mean shit
when I'm the poison.

And the others only stole my confidence,
But I'm confident enough
to end my part of the story...

Here I am standing at the edge of my damn,
I listen to my head, and it never says forfeit,
I cried streams of river,
But these tears never rolled a six.
Me trusting,
me loving,
were all my vices.

You can skip this!

The scapula moves in many ways,
Up and down and side to side,
it sways.
It can rotate and tilt as well,
These movements are important to tell,
For they help us move our arms with ease,
And perform tasks with grace and expertise.
Elevate,
depress,
protract,
Retract,
rotate up and down,
Movements of the body are exact,
muscles working all around.
Keeping your shoulder intact.

Fool me twice

Gun
Shots
Trigger
Adrenaline
In my heart
You've curved me before.
What's
Different
You Turned
My wood
Into bark
To Semblance plants
Giving birth to resemblance hydrangeas
With the powers
Of your
False
Love

SADE (PART III)

With fierce intent,
She grasps the weapon.

A phallus black as night,
Stands tall and proud in sight.
Its shape and form so bold,
A sight to behold.
It stands there firm and strong,
A symbol of power all along.
Its presence demands respect,
A sight that fills one with delight.

A ruler's measure,
so precise,
Ten inches long,
no more, no less,
A standard set,
A minimum length.

A set of harnesses,
it has indeed.

Sade was wet
Nora spoke with ease,
        "Ok, put it on."
Sade grinned,
With a smile so wide,
her joy couldn't hide.

Over Nora's head,
the strap is placed,
secure and snug,
with gentle grace.

Nora stood still,
Her mind in a haze,
Confusion clouding her thoughts,
Lost in a bewildering maze.

Before she could inquire,
Sade placed the strap over her mouth.

With a firm tug,
the straps were pulled,
Taut and secure,
they held their hold.
No room for slippage or for play,
The load was set to go its way.

Nora laid there,
Still and serene,
In peaceful repose,
A tranquil scene.

An erect form with length to spare,
But only ten inches to represent down there,
A tool for pleasure,
a toy to play,
With the bottom four inches of dildo going the other way.

Filling her mouth
With her tongue,
she tried to force it out
The strap,
it held with all its might.

Toy Story

Nipple clamps
Handcuffs
Whips
vibrator rings
Butt plugs
ball gags
an endless list of sex toys.

A set for the perfect world of orgasmic pleasure
She said you just want to sleep with me!
I just want to sleep with you, not in a sexual way
But I just want to sleep next to you
and watch Netflix,
and listen to your heartbeat,
and hear you talk about your day.

Or...
Penetrate her depth with all my might!

Dancing in the night

She is my love goddess.
While wearing a silk gown,
Her complexion glows in the light of a gorgeous sunset.
Caramel drizzled.
Her hips have curves.
To reach her thighs,
Legs are long and come to an end.
With such delicate feet,
I had to meet her on the dance floor.

Love More

Can you hear my heart...!
Synchronized with your breaths,
My world revolves around you,
witnessing the universe through your eyes,
As eternal light, I want to make you smile.
Until it stopped beating with joy.

Can you hear my soul...!
Filled with your love and charisma,
You are my dawn, that I start mornings with,
You are my moon, whom I adore from afar,
The light of your eyes I felt first,
Understand my words until tears burst.

Can you feel my thoughts...!
Collections of sweet memories,
In the dim light, your dazzling eyes and face,
Your voice in silence and smile in distress,
Your poetries in my mind and
soul in my essence,
And all I have is just you in
my subconsciousness.

All I want is to see you smile...!
It's how you filled and penetrated my soul,
Deeper in my eyes, you will finally know,
I loved you more than the love I show.

WET ENCORE

She laid face down on the bed.
As if she knew I wanted it
Her nipples pressed so slightly
against the cool sheets
Her clitoris was clearly in view
In my state of hypnosis,
Her body is redefined by purity.
My hands traced down her perishing curves.
I stroked her chords in hopes of a melody.

Fingers left moist
craving for a taste
The hourglass grew near.
So, I tied her up
and threw her back down.

She told me to bend the knee
and kiss the toe of the camel.
Holding pressurized juices

I sunk my head between her thighs.
She pushed her calves up to her cheeks.
I lovingly ran my tongue over her mound.
And continued to caress her open wound
While I mishandled her Brest
It was so clear that our chakras were aligned.
With her soul on my lips

TO BE CONTINUED...

Black Charm

My childish expression,
when I smile,
I blush with romance.
When I laugh,
I feel beautiful.
My eyes can enslave.
They can sell you the world.

Or

Nothing more.
Sexy dark brown,
Among their magnificent hues
They provide narratives of pleasure,
heartbreak,
and pain.

My brows have thick arches.
Long and graceful man lashes
beautiful teeth
pulling your heartstrings.

Cupid is powerless against me.
Charisma wants to date me.
Aphrodite is battling romance fever.
Kama desires to fuck me.
As I'm the prophet of love!

WET ENCORE II

I gave her a taste
then I moved my lips to nibble down her neck.
My bites were firm but not vicious.
Making her blush in all the right places
She then pushes me onto my back.
We continue to kiss.
Her hands bound
locking her arms around my head.
She allowed herself to sink down
the length of my brutal thickness
Slowly rising and falling.

With trimmers of orgasms
at the rhythm of her drum
I began grinding my hips.
Hooking my curve

Flipping her over to
The death position
I strummed her plum
With my thumb
and start blowing her ass right off the map.
Her hands broke free
while one hand retrains her neck.
The other was clamping her ass.

She cradled my shaft with her tongue.
Moving her neck
slowly grinding
goose bumps form
My toes become vulnerable
As she swallowed my raw emotion.

OUR LAST SUMMER

I will jump into love blindly
if it means that love will catch me.
love of another's chest that beats at a soft pace.
A love craving that is worse than any addiction
one you never settled into,
because no one tells you to stop.
Who goes into recovery for being a...
hopeless romantic?

Heat Check

Look at me while you fuck me
Take your time
Kiss me
Fuck me in rhyme
My tongue goes down your spine
passionately
While my hands intertwine
Your body is my body
We're in sync and on time
Your lips are so perfect
Press them against mine
I use my stroke to Express
to invade your mind

I fuck you, Thick
You fuck me wet
I love when you bite me,
Our sex is in its prime
I love when you excite me
Damn, I can't wait to fuck next time.

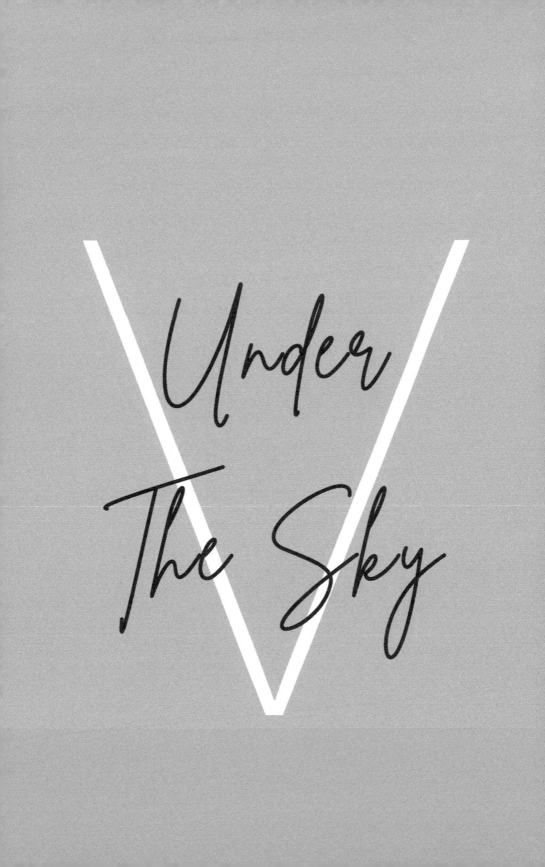

STORY TIME

"Babe, I want to go out and have dinner. Like old couples back then." Sade said getting antsy. "Why can't we just stay in and have a little fun?" James said with a grin, grabbing Sade's butt. Sade bit her lip and rolled her eyes because she knows what James wants and is teasing him. "I want to go out, baby, please. Let's go to Lulu's Diner." Sade begged He couldn't resist and gave in. James. " Okay fine, but you're doing everything I say tonight; do you understand?" He demanded. "Yes." Sade smiled "Yes, what?" James gave her a look that she can't refuse. "Yes, daddy." She said and went to get her stuff ready.

James went to grab his wallet and keys to leave. He called his wife, Nora, to let her know that he was coming home late tonight. "Hey yeah, I'm on a deadline tonight. I know it's the second time this week, but I'm so close to that bonus. Don't wait up; I love you too." Sade walks back in. As Nora hung up. "My name? Sure, um, it's James. Yes, thank you." He hung up the phone. "Babe, are you ready? I made us a reservation at Lulu's." James said.

Sade slowly makes her way across the room in a black dress, and James can't help but stare. Does it look naughty? Sade looks down at herself. James whispered, "Mmm, not at all." I assume you're not wearing underwear under that?" James hungrily scanned her from head to toe. Sade shook her head. Mmm, it's a little secret just between you and me. With a sultry wink, she sauntered over to grab her purse and head to the car. In a flash, James spun around and swept her off her feet. Why do you have to be so enticingly challenging? James questioned.

Apologies, Daddy. Would you prefer me to be obedient? Sade seduced. "Looks like someone is going to need to be punished," James said. Mmm, that's alright with me. I actually enjoy it. Sade tantalized. James grinned seductively, realizing he'd need to conjure up something more enticing. As they cruised to Lulu's, James turned on some music. Sade tried to change it, but James tapped her hand and told her no.

They arrive at the restaurant, James walks around the car to get Sade, and he hands the keys to the valet with a charming grin. "Here's a tip; we will be leaving in an hour, tops. Please make sure the car is at the front by then." He told the valet, who nodded. Are you all set and eager? James looked at Sade. "Why wouldn't I be?" Sade looked puzzled. Not knowing James had made other plans during the night, in surprising Sade but he also had another plan to get home at some point. They headed over to their table in the secluded area by the window. James and Sade indulged in a delectable feast and sipped on fine wine to quench their thirst. "Would you like dessert?" James asked Sade who was drinking from her glass. "Yes, daddy," Sade said.

James ordered her a chocolate cake with fudge and whipped cream. She was so excited. Just then, the waiter came over and told Sade he had something for her. Sade was feeling a little confused. "What's this?" Sade looked at the envelope. "I'm not sure; why don't you open it and see?" With an enticing grin, James uttered. Sade opens the envelope and finds a plane ticket for a skydiving trip. "Skydiving? James, you know I'm scared of heights." She said. "I'll be with you the whole time; if you are scared, just look at me," James reassured her, and they left the restaurant.

A few minutes later, James and Sade get to the airport for their flight. Sade gazes into James' eyes as he gives a subtle nod and smile. They are soon off in the air and flying over the country. They'll have to take the plunge soon. "Are you ready, baby?" Sade catches James' gaze and feels a shiver run down her spine. As she nods, they both lean in close to each other, ensuring their safety and igniting a fiery passion. "1...2.......3! Jump!" James yells, and they both jump out together. Sade's fingers clench around James's biceps as she closes her eyes in ecstasy. "Babe, it's okay; I've got you. Unveil those gorgeous eyes, my love. James tells her. She does not let him go. They descend sensually and shed their harnesses. Sade turns around as she still takes off the rest of her harness, not noticing James get on one knee and pull out a very shiny ring. As Sade slowly turns around, James has the biggest smile on his face.

Sade's lips parted in a gasp of surprise, and her smile revealed a hint of lure. "OMG..." She says, "Sade, I know we've had our ups and downs, and I know things haven't been perfect. But I know one thing for sure: You make me the happiest person alive, and I would never trade anything in the world for that. So, I'm begging you: will you be mine forever and ever? James inquires with a sultry tone. Sade doesn't know what to say and hesitates for a second. "Yes! I'll marry you!" Sade exclaimed in excitement.

James sweeps her off her feet with a passionate kiss, then gently places her back down and slips the ring onto her finger. "Let's get out of here, yeah?" James asks her. Sade nods, and they get in their car and head back home. Upon arriving home, my stunning fiancée, Sade, was exhausted from our passionate evening, so she retired to bed.

I never thought I would meet the most amazing girl and get engaged to her. Sade makes me the happiest person alive. I adore the way her gaze lingers on me, and I can feel the electricity between us as we share the same captivating thoughts. I crave you. My mind keeps replaying the same seductive thoughts. I'm always thinking about you, and I want you even when I'm with her. I crave your caress, your lips, your form, and Nora just can't compare to you. I've been wanting to rip your clothes off throughout the day. "Baby, wake up," I said, still rubbing her. I will caress your voluptuous curves and explore every inch of your body with my tongue. I want you all over me. I desire to bask in your passionate heat. You make me wild with lust, and eventually, I shall have my way with you.

Thinking about her sleeping in the other room made me want to go lay with her, but I couldn't because I had to get home. I was so horny that I immediately went to her room. She was wrapped in my shirt and her lacy underwear. "Babe," I whisper while rubbing her clit. "Hmm?" She softly moaned. "Baby, wake up," I said, still rubbing her. "What are you doing up here, James?" She asked. "I want you, right now." "I thought you had to go home and get ready for your business trip in the morning." She asked. I sensually slip her panties down and kiss her shirt up. Sade's attractive smile and lack of resistance only fuel my burning desire, as I know deep down, she craves me. I start to lick her clit and spit on her softly. I grab her waist and squeeze her; she grabs at my back, enjoying what my tongue and hands do.

I stroke her soft breasts and take them into my mouth, causing a soft, sensual moan from her lips. "Mmm, shh, my love," I whisper with a smirk. Sade bites her lip. I rub faster and lick her everywhere. I nibbled on her luscious thigh, and she sensually arched her back and clutched the silky sheets. "I'm about to cum!" she said out of breath in a whisper. "Don't stop, baby!" Her breathy sighs escaped her lips, a fiery sound that filled the room. I listened and didn't stop until she came. I curled two fingers inside her and rubbed it even faster as she grabbed my hair until she squirted everywhere. I passionately locked lips with her before bidding her goodnight. She wraps her arms around me and squeezes tight. "I love you. Please don't go," she pleads with a passionate voice. " I wish I didn't have to, but I do. If only I could stay with you. I love you too. James whispered and kissed her on the cheek before he left. "See you soon, babe," I say as he cover her back up and let her drift back to sleep.

Hurts, don't it

How do you admit it?
Admit that our love is rapidly diminishing?
I'm not ok!
I used to take in her comfortable scent.
She was home.
I'd miss her daily.
but for her once a month at most.
It breaks my heart to think of her with another guy.

You can act as though it doesn't matter anymore.
But that pride will leave you burnt
And your entire being bellows with rage.
Of course, life isn't fair.

It's incredible how love can appear unexpectedly.
Suppose you fall out of love
just as you realize you were in it.
When you feel like crying in deep arguments!
Just looking at her could bring on the tears.
Is it because I'm nostalgic for us?
or because I'm still in love?

The Darkest Moment

I finally got my life back on track,
one step forward, three steps back.
I give thanks to me.
Myself.
Because you see this self,
Has not had it easy,
It was uneasy.
But despite that tough cup,
I drank form, I never gave up.

The whispers did not get to me.
Well, they almost did a number on me
But quickly my senses came back
I know where I come from,
Highland Hills!

Over time, there
We built armor.
A tough armor.
For that reason, on this planet,
The words, those bullets,
that were aimed so perfectly,
You know what, thankfully?
They missed properly!
They missed with accuracy,
An accuracy that puts opps to shame.
Because they were aimed to defame.
At the wrong person.

Pins & Needles

Considering it all,
I wish my touch was felt.
Reminiscing about times
when we moved around.

The fatigue feeling of your calves,
don't sound so bad now.
Our chemistry,
Basketball,
jumping in the air.
Our competitiveness was so close.

The bittersweetness of heat,
Not being able to take the cold.
As our dance moves,
no longer cut rugs
and distance disappears.
I can't feel your control,
The sadness is insane.
We will never become vertical.
as I took you for granted.

I get in my chair.
I put you guys closer
I'm deeply impaled by my strength.
You made me tall.
Now I feel small.
Two soul mates,
Together,
we remain.

Morning Tunes

I intend to be the cause of your morning joy.
I desire to be the foundation of your pleasure.
The tune on your tongue
The swing in your step
You are indeed the harmony on my lips.
The enthusiasm in my hips

Shiver

She was stunned by a chill in the air.
Her intuition was sending out negative energy.
She felt nauseated and tried to sleep again.
Arched and breathing sharply.
The room was pitch black.
Deafeningly quiet.
Something felt strange.
She found herself wanting to look into it.
But was too tired to move.
That evening was gloomy.
Eventually she raised her head to wipe her eyes
And glanced at the clock.
Her anxiety level rose slightly.
while she didn't notice him watching her.

Do better!

True aggravation
Being disappointed
By your person,
The difference-maker that
didn't make a difference.

Opened up my heart
Because I thought you were the one

It's funny
You were never meant to mean this much
You did your job though
You caught me
When I fell into the pool of your heart
That I could have drowned in,
But no!

That feeling of being so deep under water
Holding my breath to the last second
before giving up.
Swimming closer to the surface
before you pulled me out

That's what keeps me holding on
Because it's painful to let you go

SADE (PART IV)

Sade sipped from her glass,
Her lips touched the rim,
The liquid flowed within,
A moment of bliss.

With a firm grip,
He seized the shaft and held it tight,
Ready for the task.

With a sudden motion,
The hand begins to move,
In a rhythmic motion,
The pleasure starts to groove.

Nora's unease grew,
A discomfort she couldn't subdue.

She stood there,
unsure and perplexed,
She braced herself for what lay in store.

She closed her lids,
And let the darkness in.
        "I can do this," she thought.
With determination in her heart.
No obstacle could stop her,
No challenge could tear her apart.
        Sade said, "I'm going to enjoy this."
Her lower limbs, pressed with care,
Against Sade's cheek, soft and fair.
Following that, they locked eyes.

Nora's heart was filled with fear,
Yet fascination held her nearby.

With a playful touch,
Sade carried out Teasing herself with the tip,
A tantalizing game she did employ
As she explored her own sweet joy.

Allowing for the initial inch to start the race,
A chance to move at a steady pace.

Up and down,
penetrating deep A rhythm that her heart does
to keep A dance of motion,
a steady beat Penetrating,
never to retreat.

With every move,
Nora felt the weight,
A burden that she couldn't shake,
A pressure that she couldn't break.

Nearer drew her swollen pearl,
A sight that caused Nora chills
Aching for the touch of pleasure's swirl.

With A serpent-like form,
it wraps Coiling tight,
Stretching around the shaft
Sade settled in

gagging, Nora grabbed Sade's ass
As Sade sunk down the length of the shaft

it was like a painting
A series of strokes
A sequence of lines in graceful motion.
A dance divine.
A canvas alive, With colors and light,
A masterpiece born,
Each stroke so bright.

Steady was the tempo,
A rhythm unbroken,
A beat that kept time.

Her legs were locked in place,
A grip so tight and strong,
But then she let them go,
And Nora's freedom came along.

Sade started to drive deeper
Bouncing on her face
A curious sight,
A physical moment,
Bringing delight.

There was about to be A climax,
dramatic and grand,
Was about to unfold,
unplanned.

Leaving a creamy wave
Trembling legs, Sade rose,
Her body weary, her spirit tough.

She flopped on her back,
Giggling without a lack.

Nora's bag, she did inspect,
To find her phone,
all lit and decked.

A presence felt,
A figure seen,
Someone was there,
Or so it seemed.

With attentive ear he heard it all,
And then, with measured words,
he spoke.
"You need to come home!"

To be continued...

4th and 1

Success is a test.
Believe in yourself.
Forget the rest
You will make a dime.
But first, dream big.
Let your passion shine.
Innovation is an endless quest.
Challenge the status quo.
And do it with your chest.
You never know.
Your business could be good.
Take a chance
If it changes your world, then you should
follow your heart.
Your head could
leave you at start.

Green Brownie

Domesticated paradise
Blue Kool-Aid
swallow the pill.
Her rosy lips.
The adversity.
How do you feel?

2000s

What if the stars
And the sky presented a show?
We sit in my driveway.
To talk for hours
This feeling can grow!

PEN-DEMIC

My love language
is no language
on this earth
with enough words
that can articulate
What I feel
How I feel
When I think of you
Inside
where I shower
Pieces
of my mind
that I try in a vain attempt
to release

Desire

Touching your hand is something I enjoy.
In a very real way,
it's a bridge to your very essence.
Reminds me of the unique connection we share
A hoped-for reality
An unsaid truth
It's a pure,
unscripted
affection
Eternal
Love

Beautiful curls

As a kid, I dreamt of this day.
I think I owe myself an apology.
Because that dream did no justice to you, my love.
To my feelings for you, my love.
Thinking of it now, I missed a lot.
In detail.

I am able to forgive myself because of you,
Because, as I look into your eyes now,
all I see is you.
I would never want the dream I dreamt,
In my childhood
to become true, as it was an understatement,
Because it never described your gorgeous smile,
And those eyes, too, were left out.
I only had a silhouette.

These feelings I have can only be felt.
Not dreamt.
Touching you can only be felt.
Not dreamt.
The thud in my heart as I look at you,
Only increases
And I know I need to slow down,
But I cannot!

What others said about love,
was just a gist,
And that was not enough
to prepare me for when I fell deeply for you.
But I am glad
because of the journey of discovering you
Was worth it, an adrenaline jerker.
So, you, my love, are mine.
May the heavens seal this union.
To eternity.

The first goodbye

To be continued
A story left untold
leaves us hanging
With questions to behold.
What happens next?
We eagerly await
The next chapter,
To seal our fate.
The plot thickens.
As we hold our breath,
To be continued,
Brings us closer to death.
But fear not,
For the story lives on,
To be continued,
until the final dawn.